NOTHING WRONG ANYMORE

A MANUAL FOR SPIRITUAL JANITORS

FELIPE OLIVEIRA

– INDEX –

– PREAMBLE –

"In my early twenties, driven by a desire for liberation from inner turmoil and suffering, I sought refuge in a 4th Way school in the Gurdjieff-Ouspensky tradition. This experience granted me invaluable insights into the compartments and workings of the human psyche.

A pivotal moment came when a friend handed me a book by John Wheeler, which catalyzed a Revelation or Awakening during intense emotional hardship. In a moment of spontaneous inquiry for "the truth of I," a vast ocean of Pure Consciousness was discovered where no separate self existed. Peace coexisted with pain.

I then embarked on a two-year pilgrimage, meeting teachers and absorbing their teachings. Yet, as the non-duality paradigm began to feel arid and lifeless, a new question emerged: "Why exactly does the ego create so much unnecessary suffering? And how?"

This inquiry led me to the Michael Teachings and the tools of Traditional Horary Astrology and Marseilles Tarot. Armed with these wisdom systems, I delved deep into the intricacies of the ego, leaving no stone unturned. As Nisargadatta Maharaj once said, "The mind must be known." In my case, this thorough investigation proved to be the key.

Eventually, the sense of separation dissolved, and the psychological suffering and seeking ceased, imbuing life with a quiet but profound simplicity beyond the mind's egoic, as well as metaphysical and spiritual complexities. In this space, nothing is inherently wrong – all is but a dream, and I Am.

In the essays and dialogues that follow, I share what I've learned and unlearned in the winding as well as the direct paths. My offer is to illuminate the mental-emotional mechanisms of self-imposed limitations and hint at the peace that lies beyond them." – Felipe

"Not this, or that.
Rest
All is a dream
Peace at last."

— Narayan

– Spirit –

– WHAT IS ENLIGHTENMENT?

In my definition, it is a revelation or recognition. It is recognized that the True Nature of Reality is Pure Consciousness and that I am not separate from It.

That recognition can have many consequences in the life of the person to whom it happened. Most notably, it heralds the beginning of the last stretch of the spiritual path for some, and it is the actual end of the path for some.

The word Enlightenment is symbolic. Before Enlightenment, it was dark, so Reality could not be seen, revealed, or recognized. With Enlightenment, light is present, and Reality becomes visible.

The word Awakening is likewise symbolic of the same event. In sleep, Reality cannot be discerned. In wakefulness, it can.

The revelation or recognition is impersonal. Nobody awakens, is awake, or is enlightened.

— I find that hard to understand.

It is not hard to understand; it is impossible. The intellect cannot grasp its Source. The intellect is the brush; the Source is the painter. Once the seeking bug bites, the only resolution is Enlightenment itself. After Enlightenment, if doubt and seeking persist, paying attention and eliminating the useless can help bring about Realization.

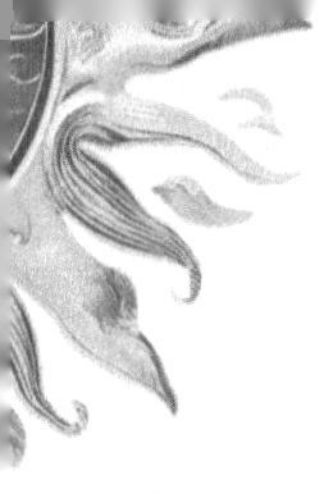

The intellect can function both in favor or against Enlightenment and Realization.

Some spiritual ideas that help strengthen the personality early on the path function against Enlightenment and Realization later.

What I am sharing with you is to help the intellect operate favorably toward both Enlightenment and Realization by aligning it with how things are, eliminating unclear, malformed, inapplicable, or false ideas, and eliminating false beliefs. From there, attention can flow in unexpected and surprising ways.

– What is there?

An Ocean without beginning or end. Still, incorruptible, unchanging, uncaused, un-manifested. Potential.

When manifested, the world is there, as mind. Waves appear as movements and shapes in the Ocean. A unified appearance as a seamless single timeless experience. Still Ocean.

The world is an appearance, and the body and the personality are part of the world, not something separate from it.

The world is equal to mind. This is not an analogy. Mind is not a box or container. Mind is the present projection of the perceivable world.

Mind has its source in Pure Consciousness, and it is projected like a film on Pure Consciousness.

AFTER AWAKENING, THE TERM SEEKER IS NO LONGER APPLICABLE.

If we must entertain a concept of self, "seeker" is not helpful, for what should be obvious reasons after Awakening.

The seeker seeks something. Awakening has made it clear that what was sought is nothing that can be obtained; there is no one seeking and no one who can get it.

Instead of seeking self-realization, grab a brush, soap, and a bucket. Put on your janitor uniform and do what janitors do. This personality and body are not required to do anything else after the Revelation.

The "way of denial" is not an abstract notion that spiritual people can pick and choose from the esoteric library shelf.

The way of denial is what is required after Awakening happens. It is a known pattern in spiritual development. The central process is elimination, removal, and cleaning up.

If Awakening has happened and there is a felt need to do something, then the right tool is a broom and just enough guidance, inquiry, or meditation to be clear on which rugs to lift and sweep under.

– Is Awakening a Gradual Process?

Awakening is not a process; it is an event. It is a revelation, and what is revealed in It is beyond time.

However, the personality, as a whole, and the ego undergo a process both before and after that event.

In fact, two different processes take place.

The first process is accumulation, growth, control, and effort. It is preparatory work performed primarily before Awakening.

After Awakening, the process of elimination begins. As the mind becomes clearer of wrong beliefs, wrong ideas, unfounded fears, and the various negative emotions fear spawns, the peace of Total Acceptance pervades our daily lives more and more.

– Can Enlightenment be transmitted directly to other people?

Consciousness is not susceptible to movement, location, ownership, or stewardship. It is not some thing, not even a subtle or metaphysical thing. So it does not move from one person to another.

However, words, a look, or just the presence of a person can elicit Recognition or Insight in another person. That can certainly happen. Recognition can also occur by reading a book, watching a video, or totally out of the blue.

What is recognized is shared among all individuals and thus precludes the concept of transmission.

What is recognized is what we are, and all is, not anything we have. It is not something God, gods, saints, ascended masters, gurus, and "enlightened people" have and are out to dispense and transmit.

The personification, ownership, understanding, or control of Consciousness is the intellect trying to put it in a jar. This does not lead to liberation from suffering.

So, at some point, we go to teachers. If the teacher does their job, and the seeker is ripe, the imagination that enlightened people have something that you don't is destroyed. That opens the door to the release of suffering.

– It is said that there are many Awakenings or glimpses.

From all of the Awakenings or glimpses, only one is significant. That is where it is irrevocably clear that Consciousness is all there is and that there is no such thing as "I" separate from Consciousness. That is the only Awakening that deserves the name of Awakening.

That is a revelation of Truth, and Truth will allow the eradication of the lie of separation arising in the ego and the unnecessary suffering that that lie produces. That is what is meant by the saying, "The Truth shall set you free."

For a blessed few people, there is evidence that Awakening is simultaneous with the death of the sense of separation in the ego. For the rest of us mortals, they are two different events. One opens a door, and the other burns the door down.

The Truth revealed in Awakening becomes the point of reference for ongoing and renewed psychological development in terms of releasing of suffering.

As that reference point from Awakening becomes more present in our daily lives, and more nonsense is eliminated from our intellect and emotions, the more that Truth imbues peace into our lives.

– DOES THE "I" GET UNIFIED WITH THE TOTALITY IN THE END?

No. There is no "I" that is separate.

That separation is an unexamined assumption that about seven billion people go for without a second thought.

So, any spiritual idea concocted around that assumption is either pointless imagination or geared toward a specific type of seeker early on the path.

For a mature seeker, it is stated that what we call "I" is a concept associated with a personality, ego, and body and has a practical function in life. But it was never separate from Consciousness.

Awakening is the event when that assumption is uncovered. Self-inquiry or Self-remembering is the act of challenging that assumption. Spiritual Realization is when it is destroyed, and nothing takes its place; thus, nothing is wrong anymore.

– DO WE WAKE UP TO THE DREAM OR FROM THE DREAM?

It is assumed that there is a separate entity that can awaken either to or from the dream.

There isn't such an entity. It is an unexamined assumption. That is the very fact that is revealed in Awakening.

There is an Awakening. The Awakening reveals in no uncertain terms that no one awakens or is awake. And the dream itself is irrelevant.

We are Consciousness. Consciousness is not conscious "of" anything. Neither are "we" inside Consciousness. Consciousness IS everything.

There is no separate subject experiencing the dream, and there is no actual subject in the dream except as a mental construct and the experience of the senses.

Subject-object relationships ARE the dream. So, an "I" who supposedly awakens to or from the dream is part of the dream.

Also, there is not a problem with the dream being a dream.

Usually, we want to awaken because our dream is unpleasant. Fair enough. That is the basis of suffering and seeking.

However often, we want to escape the pain by idealizing bliss, preferably eternal, somewhere outside the dream. We are unhappy and suffering and then project a "spiritual" solution.

That idealism remains unfulfilled as there is no end of seeking or suffering down that road.

The personality is the dream. The mind, the emotions, the world are the dream. It is the manifested. Pleasure and pain. It is fine as it is.

The dream is not a problem. That is precisely why Spiritual Realization can be expressed as "there is nothing wrong anymore."

– MR. X SAYS HE WOKE UP AND IS NOW AWAKE. BUT YOU SAID NOBODY WAKES UP.

Maybe it is a question of language and semantics, maybe not. I have no way to tell. So, you have to figure out where he is coming from by yourself. Ask him to explain what he means; that is what teachers are there for.

What I can offer you is to speak from my experience.

In my way of speaking about Awakening, I cannot say "I woke up". It simply is not true.

I never was asleep, and I never woke up. And I know that that is the same for You, and for Mr. X, for that matter. You are not the body; you are not the personality. The body and personality do sleep and wake up. You do not. Reflect on this.

In my experience, there was an event that could be called Awakening. That event revealed, among other facets, that no one awakens. A misunderstanding about what we call "I" or "self" is exposed, and what is left is Things as They Are.

The person imagines they will awaken. Awakening occurs and destroys that imagination.

Spiritually speaking, "I" or "being awake" are meaningless concepts in my current experience. They are irrelevant to Things as They Are.

The main reason I speak about these things is because such an Awakening heralds the end of suffering and the end of seeking. So, I think it is a worthwhile subject to talk about, considering that I suffered for forty-some years and some people did help me to clarify where my vision was blurred and open the door to Awakening.

A person does not awaken or become enlightened. Awakening or Enlightenment happens "to a person". And what is revealed is beyond the person—our True Nature.

– It seems that Spiritual Realization allows us to live comfortably in our own skins...

There is Total Acceptance of who we are as a person, including our character defects and bad habits.

But to avoid a possible misunderstanding, I would not use the word "comfortably." I would say it allows us to live with a certain tranquility.

If we have financial security, health, a home, a support group, and are surrounded by beauty and other nice things life has the potential to provide, yes, living comfortably is appropriate. If those things are lacking, it can be very uncomfortable indeed.

Spiritual Realization does not solve money, health, or relationship problems, and they do not just vanish as if by magic. Seeking a spiritual solution to non-spiritual problems indicates a fundamental misunderstanding about what kind of suffering ceases upon Spiritual Realization.

Perfection is an uneducated ego's fantasy. This is a subtle point in the "spiritual ego" that, if resolved, may end seeking and reveal that there is Nothing Wrong.

That misunderstanding is often the final obstacle. The ego must be known in all of its subtle manifestations. No stone can be left unturned.

– Is Spiritual Realization the Death of the Ego?

It depends on one's definition of ego. In my definition the ego is the sense of self that allows us to function in life. If it were to die before this body dies we would become invalids.

The notion of a dead ego seems like an egoic strategy spurred by the desire to push away or eliminate something we do not like or that causes us trouble.

Many of us have an overemotional or moral response to the ego and then create an enemy to despise, denigrate, complain about, fight against, and ultimately kill, both in ourselves and others.

However, with the dissolving of the sense of separation, the ego and its responses to stimuli become a non-issue. It becomes irrelevant. There is no one to care. That is the death that takes place. The "ego problem" we once had dies and does not resurrect. What a relief! Peace at last!

– EVERYTHING IS AN ILLUSION...

A minute ago, you told me you are still suffering. You may repeat that everything is an illusion and continue suffering.

That does not help. The mind is unfocused and adrift. That idea is a blunt tool and can be safely discarded.

The root of psychological suffering is an illusion, that is for sure. But simply saying that is of no use either. Seeking and suffering will continue until that is realized in direct experience, and its truth pervades the mind deeply enough.

Investigate and find the root.

– WHY DOES RAMANA MAHARSHI SAY THERE IS NO "OTHER"?

My educated guess is that a particular seeker needed to hear that at that moment to shake off the wrong belief that the person is a separate entity and, in doing so, release the seeker from psychological suffering and establish Impersonal Stillness.

There is no separate "I" entity, neither for the sage nor for anyone else. Therefore, the other is a concept like "I." It is useful and necessary for practical and functional purposes but irrelevant and obstructing in terms of Self-Knowledge.

– ARE YOU SAYING THE PERSON DOES NOT EXIST?

It does not exist as a separate entity. However, as a network of present thoughts and emotions associated with a body, yes, of course, it exists. We would not be having this conversation if that were not the case.

We call the person "I" for purely practical purposes so that we can experience certain aspects of duality. That does not imply or mean that "I" is a separate entity from the Whole.

That is an assumption, a fundamental error of judgment humans experience which, at some point, propels spiritual work to initiate. It is the mother of all misunderstandings.

The person is one of the many objects that appear in and arise out of the Consciousness that We Are.

– How do you know the state of our Essential Nature that you experience is not a passing state?

Because the very nature of the Essential State engenders the effortless conviction that there is no "I" who experiences or can experience it, and because it is Not Two, there is no opposite to it. Therefore, there is no passing any more than there is a coming.

What comes and goes and changes for the seeker is the intensity of the sense of separation.

The entire seeking drama and the motivation for Satsang are based on the assumption that you will get to some state and be there permanently. This assumption is a false belief that springs out of the sense of separation.

"Spirit" is not an experience 'we have'.

– I find that hard to grasp.

Rightfully so. It is ungraspable.

– How can we understand it and reach the peace you talk about?

We can't understand it. We can only understand experience. The source of experience is non-understandable. But that is only half of the pointer. Some people may well "get it" by hearing only that half. Lucky ones, those are.

There is the other half for the rest of us mortals: we cannot understand Truth, but we can understand what is false. Look at the false, recognize it as false, and it dissolves naturally and effortlessly, and Truth "becomes known."

When we are children, we believe in Santa Claus. One day, we discover that it does not exist, so its falsehood dissolves forever. It is impossible to reinstate Santa Claus. You live free from that falsehood and its harmless implications, although it can disappoint some children.

So, the pointer is given: look into your experience and find "I." Where is it? Focus on the inquiry. Look carefully.

If you look from the correct angle, you will see that "I" is exactly like Santa Claus: an image or concept, but in this case, associated with a body and a personality. This is not an analogy. The process of seeing the false as false is exactly the same.

The problem is that we have accumulated an enormous network of beliefs, habits, and justifications about who or what we are since childhood, including spiritual teachings such as those that teach us that "we are" a soul in evolution.

We have developed a serious emotional stake in this "I," which poses a considerable obstacle to the realization of Peace. The implications of this falsehood are far from harmless, like Santa Claus's.

So, the work is to study the mind, stop justifying our petty negative emotions because they function like glue for the psyche, and stop repeating wrong beliefs. Then, the recognition may arise that all those thoughts, emotions, and sensations do not equate with "I" in any way at all.

If we keep at it and keep discarding the false, what is left is the non-understandable Peace of Being.

– It is said that "there is no world and nothing ever happened". What's that got to do with Self-Realization?

Notionally, consciousness has two modes of being: Manifested and Un-manifested. But they are concurrent and not separate. They are not two. There is no division or movement between them.

Within this paradigm, all that can be experienced, including thoughts, emotions, and perceptions of any kind in any dimension, physical and beyond, is called the Manifested.

As the Un-manifested, Consciousness is pure potential and thus can be said to be the source of the Manifested. It is dimensionless, therefore timeless and spaceless. Thus, there is no world, and nothing ever happened, is happening, or will happen. It is ever-present, perfect stillness brimming with life.

This is a description of how things are now and at all times. Consciousness "is".

We will not be free when "there is no world, and nothing ever happened." That is a misunderstanding. It is the intellect projecting. Enough of projections. Let go of these ideas.

We have to discern when the ego is playing tricks and using spiritual ideas such as these to project happiness "outside of the manifestation," "outside the dream," "beyond," or in "heaven," as if the Manifestation was a problem in itself. And to solve that problem, we would abandon it and go into the Un-manifested. That is imagination and over-intellectualization and is probably a sign of depression or boredom.

It is better to acknowledge one is unhappy and focus on studying the psyche and the ego more thoroughly.

We have to be aware of where thoughts come from in our personalities. Use the right tool for the problem we are faced with and leave the Un-manifested and the Manifested alone.

– WHAT IS THE SENSE "I AM?"

You may have had the experience of waking up in the morning before your eyes open, and you do not know where you are. There is only infinite dark space, but it appears illuminated, and the light shines from "you." There is no thought, emotion, or sensation; you do not have a name, and you are no one.

The awareness of "existing." That is the "I Am". The only knowledge that is present is the knowledge that you are. It is not known conceptually but directly in Consciousness as pure Consciousness manifested.

"I Am" is the seed of the world. It is the Creative principle manifested. It is the Christ Consciousness or Son of God. The Creation out of the Creator. Manifestation out of the Un-manifested.

Metaphysically speaking, space appears first in Creation, followed by the element Fire: light. Let there be light.

After that, thoughts and images arise in the mind—even before the eyes open. Imagination arises. That is the element Air. It arises after Fire. So, the world appears layer by layer.

Next, emotions appear—the element Water. Memories and emotional connections begin to stir. After emotions, sensations, and the body are felt, thus awareness of the physical world arises. That is the element Earth.

That is the cosmology. This model can be seen depicted in many Eastern and Western traditional esoteric diagrams.

Psychologically, if the sense of separation is active, psychological suffering likely arises due to repeated patterns of thinking, feeling, and sensations over the years.

This creates the impression that something is not quite right about life——a subtle inquietude, and often not subtle at all.

Most people then enter a state where there is no more questioning; there is only repetition of misperceptions and wrong ideas about reality. So, psychological suffering is inevitable and persisting.

With adequate inquiry, we can begin to look inward. The Truth is not hidden. Only a particular aspect of the mind is apparently obscuring it. Once we observe what is happening well, the attachment from our erroneous views falls away naturally.

The central wrong belief is in the veracity of a separate entity called "I." "I Am" is an actual creation but not a separate entity. It is Pure Consciousness manifesting spontaneously and subsequently taking the form of this personality and body. Pure Consciousness does not need to be saved, fixed, evolve, or go to paradise.

"The spiritual warrior has no outside enemies...
The spiritual warrior has no inside enemies...
The spiritual warrior has no enemies...
The spiritual warrior is in no war...
The spiritual warrior has found peace...
The spiritual warrior is no warrior...
The spiritual warrior is laughing...
The spiritual warrior is...
The warrior is...
Spirit..."

— Narayan

- PSYCHE -

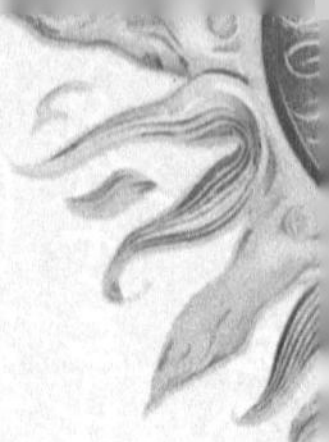

– WHAT IS SELF-REMEMBERING?

In my definition, self-remembering is the act of directing attention to the source of attention.

An archer must know where the target is before they can shoot the arrow. We must know what the Self is before it can be remembered. Logically, Self-remembering becomes effective and efficient after Awakening, not before.

The haphazard "states of presence" that happen before Awakening are quickly claimed by the ego. "I was present", we say. "I remembered myself," we say.

The state is already gone when the thought "I am remembering myself" arises. (So to speak, because it is not really gone. What is gone is the "ego vacation," as the ego is now back making imaginary claims about "I" and consciousness).

Upon Awakening, those statements lose all meaning. They feel like a lie. And they are. No one remembers the Self. Awakening changes the paradigm of self-reference. We are not what we thought we were all along. That is why Awakening is called Awakening.

The True Self cannot be approached conceptually. It can, as the term suggests, be remembered. The act of remembering appears to begin in the mind. Soon, it becomes clear that the remembering originates beyond the mind and never really leaves its origin. It is a quiet miracle. The Self playing the game of remembering the Self. The Self calling the Self to be itself. In Tarot, this is depicted by the card "The Judgement."

The term "remembering," although far from being literally true, is apt as a pointer because it implies that the Self already "is" and that it is already known. Nothing new is being discovered or created. Only an adjustment to the angle of perception or flow of attention is needed to put an end to the sense of separation.

If that happens, no more remembering is needed, as it becomes irrevocably clear that there is no self to be remembered at all, only Pure Consciousness and We Are That—now, always, and everywhere.

– ISN'T BECOMING CONSCIOUS THE FINAL AIM OF SPIRITUALITY?

Regarding Spiritual Realization, we must see the personality in its entirety. No stone can be left unturned. All devils must come to light. All that produces suffering must be seen—no exceptions.

It is not a question of intentionally getting rid of anything; it is a question of awareness. From there, everything takes care of itself. Consciousness spontaneously eliminates what is useless.

Being conscious is not the end of the path; it is the beginning of the end. The end of the path is losing what we once believed we were.

– SOME TEACHINGS EXHORT US TO BE PRESENT. IS THAT USEFUL?

What is it that is present? What is the true nature of Presence? What is the place of the mind in Presence? Who is present in the Presence? Where is "I" in Presence? Is it the "I" that later tells our friends that "I was present"?

It is good to try to be present, but the inquiry has to go deeper to put an end to the path and suffering.

Only the realization in direct experience of what is present and what is absent in that Presence can open the door to the release of consciousness from the wheel of imagination and psychological suffering.

The Present is not a moment between the past and the future.

Time plays a role in physics and manipulation of experience and in experience itself. But physics is not the study or the pursuit of Reality.

Well, some scientists may be pursuing Reality. Still, they are taking the scenic route because they are trying to grasp Consciousness through conceptualization and measurement, which cannot be done.

Spiritually, time or any other dimension never existed; therefore, it is said nothing ever happened in Pure Consciousness. The True Nature of Reality is dimensionlessness.

The word "eternity" is often misused when speaking of spirituality because it usually implies infinite time for "me" to experience.

Presence, however, is Timelessness, not a present point in time or infinite points in time. When the realization of Who We Are takes place, that is "understood" rather clearly, and it is impossible to "un-understand" it, just like it is impossible to re-instate Santa Claus as the bringer of gifts at Christmas.

A corollary of that Understanding is that the suffering based on the necessity of "me" in the future or in the past becomes absent.

– CAN YOU COMMENT ON WHAT IS MEANT BY THE WAY OF DENIAL?

The way of denial is what happens after Awakening. In Awakening the only Thing that matters becomes Known. From then onward, most of what filled our minds about spirituality becomes obsolete and is naturally discarded because many spiritual ideas support seeking. It is that simple.

After Awakening, the idea of acquiring something, like acquiring consciousness, for example, becomes absurd.

In some traditions, the way of denial is referred to as Neti-Neti. Not this, not that. What is being sought is not anything that can be named or has a form.

In Marseilles Tarot, that pattern on the spiritual path is eloquently depicted by the card number 13, which appears immediately after the card symbolizing a Revelation or Awakening.

Eliminate. Not this, not that. What is sought is not your name, body, or "me," not "I," not Buddha, not anyone, not anything. Not your image of yourself.

After Awakening, elimination is the focus. Achievement or acquisition is imagination or entertainment. The final and only obstacle to Spiritual Realization is imagination. So, a particular form of imagination has to be eventually eliminated. The "liberated I" is an image, a projection.

– Is Spiritual Realization happiness?

Yes, as long as you are not passing a kidney stone, do not have some debilitating illness, a loved one has not just died, you have financial security and a support group, you live surrounded by nature or beauty, you are not in jail, you are not homeless, you do not live in a war zone, or you are a saint. Otherwise, Spiritual Realization is unhappiness.

This is kind of tongue-in-cheek. The word "happiness" is very biased. The degree of emotional and sensory dualism associated with it is enormous. I am not very fond of using it to point at what is Non-dual.

One of the common obstacles during seeking is the desire or longing for a state of permanent pleasure. No matter whether the pleasure is sex, coffee, or a mystical state of union with whatever we imagine god to be. It is not possible.

That naïveté dies with the death of the sense of separation. Life becomes raw, in a way. You enjoy the light breeze and the sunshine, and you are swept and crushed by a storm and everything in between.

Happiness arising from the non-compulsion to satisfy desires is different from happiness arising from satisfying desires or avoiding pain.

– Are you saying you arrived at the end of the spiritual path?

There was a chapter in my life called "a path," but no one traversed it. That is not an analogy. It is literal.

In my definition, Spiritual Realization is the removal of the false belief in the existence of a separate entity called "I" who would have left the Source and would get somewhere and find happiness.

The Happiness sought can be found but not in the way we imagined. It is Simplicity, Normalcy, and Tranquility, the same simplicity present in a three-year-old child.

The removal of the sense of separation is what is meant by the saying, "To enter the kingdom of heaven, we have to become like a little child."

However, the psyche continues learning, unlearning, adapting, desiring, creating, etc., both in physical form and beyond. That is in the very nature of human consciousness, so there is a path of what could be called evolution in time.

Some refer to the path of evolution as the spiritual path. I do not. The experience of individuality elicits that concept to describe the perception of time, learning, mastery, achievement, and creation.

While the experience of time is built into spiritual seeking, Spiritual Realization is transcendent of time or achievement.

FEAR IS AT THE CORE OF FALSE PERSONALITY.

It is the mother of all self-centered negative emotions. If fear is not seen and understood clearly, deeply, and sincerely enough, false personality remains active and in the forefront. There is no freedom there. We are stuck between hell and purgatory.

The dominance of false personality can be due to many reasons and should not be judged lightly. But seeking Enlightenment or simply longing for freedom without scrutinizing the mind is wasteful and naïve. Time is limited; use it or lose it.

Fear is intrinsically linked to the root of suffering. Having a clear understanding of fear using an objectively accurate system of psychological delineation is extremely useful. It can be very effective in neutralizing false personality and the useless suffering it produces.

Without this neutralization, any lasting peace arising from Awakening or Spiritual Realization is bound to remain unstable or simply unfulfilled.

– How do you view trauma in relation to Spiritual Realization?

Unconscious trauma or karmic events must be brought to the light of consciousness for conscious digestion. The processing itself is different for different people and different events.

The digestion could take one minute of weeping, months of psychotherapy, or a session of Ayahuasca. It does not matter. What matters is that if things stay in the dark, they will keep causing unconscious suffering until they are correctly processed with clarity, compassion, and all the necessary forgiveness.

This applies to both trauma that we suffered and trauma that we caused others, as guilt and blame are definite obstacles to Spiritual Realization.

If we know we have a sore spot in the back of our minds, it makes no sense to sit and wait. It is wise to seek methods of becoming conscious of what happened in the past to some degree and process it consciously.

Genuine pain experienced unconsciously produces unconscious, unnecessary suffering, eventually becoming calcified in the personality. The way out of that psychic hole is through light.

FALSE PERSONALITY IS THAT PART OF OUR EGO THAT, WHEN ACTIVE, PRODUCES PSYCHOLOGICAL SUFFERING.

False personality manifests through seven known and discernible patterns of fear. Knowing which patterns are our favorite means of creating suffering is helpful. These patterns form the chief obstacles to living in peace, fearlessly, and free from false expectations.

The following terms are borrowed from The Michael Teachings' Overleaves System. In that system, they are referred to as false personality's "chief features."

STUBBORNNESS
Fear of change, fear of instability, hardheadedness, willfulness, rigidity, unwillingness to accept the new, inability to change opinions, and restlessness due to unpredictable people and life situations that elicit change.

IMPATIENCE
Fear of missing out on opportunities. Fear of lack of time. Attempts to cram more activity than is possible or wise within the allotted time. Hurry. Intolerance. Irritation. Anxiety.

MARTYRDOM
Fear of being oppressed. Seeks situations where victimization is likely to occur. Pointless self-sacrifice. Excessive complaint. Feeling victimized. Somebody or the universe is "always against me." "Why does this always happen to me?"

ARROGANCE
Fear of being judged and condemned. Seeks situations where judgment is likely. Shyness. Extreme attempt not to make mistakes. Hiding. Fear of being disliked or misunderstood.

SELF-DEPRECATION
Fear of being inadequate. Fear of conflict. Fear of not being able to please. Acquiescing. Saying yes when one should say no. Low self-worth, self-abasement. Feelings of unworthiness. Inaction.

GREED
Fear of lack. Fear of loss. Accumulation of goods, knowledge, money, or experiences beyond usefulness. Hoarding. Gluttony. Stinginess. Feeling one never has enough. Dissatisfaction.

SELF-DESTRUCTION
Fear of losing or not having control. Seeks situations of danger, challenges, or great difficulty. Disregard and disdain for life. Addictions of all kinds.

– I FEEL RESTLESS MOST OF THE TIME...

Keeping neurological problems or too much caffeine aside, if restlessness persists, it probably means that false personality has not been fully seen and acknowledged. One part of the psyche wants freedom; another part wants to hide and keep suffering.

In other words, certain fearful mental-emotional patterns still get activated and run the show. Those parts of the ego are unconsciously justified in our thoughts based solely on some subtle fear that remains active and unknown.

The seven patterns of fear have been known for millennia. Find yours. We cannot bypass psychology because the psyche expresses wisdom, love, and beauty. If the psyche is encumbered by fear, it cannot express these.

The idea is not to get rid of fear but to recognize it for what it is and see whether it is justified. The fear in false personality is based on imagination. When it is seen, it dissolves.

Introspection, meditation, and analysis can be used to scrutinize the personality and determine what is true and false about its operation.

– Some say that there is nothing to be done about Enlightenment…

If there is doubt about whether something needs to be done, then something can be done because seeking is active.

So the pointer is given about the "doer," not the "doing." Where is the doer? A simple question to invite introspection. Where does the doing arise from? Period. Nothing more than that.

Performing introspection is "doing something". Not performing introspection is doing something else. There is plenty of doing. But where is the doer?

If the realization that there is no separate doer arises, that is a blessing because it will be noticed that unnecessary suffering is absent in the reality of Pure Consciousness.

Take guilt, for example. Feeling remorse for misbehaving is healthy. That is how humans learn. But guilt involves attachment to being a separate entity and adds a layer of unnecessary suffering.

The person who feels guilty suffers significantly from the inability to change one's feelings. The realization that there is no doer dissolves that suffering on the spot.

From then on, from the vantage point of impersonal witnessing, if false personality rears its head, it is perceived as a cloud passing by and not something that must be eliminated.

The Basics

Take care of the body and physical needs. Otherwise, it may be difficult to discern between real and imaginary suffering.

Be creative and materialize that creativity. That includes finding solutions to problems. Or else one may become susceptible to depression and rejection of life.

Find tools and methods to uncover and process past trauma. That includes discernment and awareness of trauma in those you share your life with as they will influence you. Interact with sane and sensitive people and expose your inner life to them, as that will provide perspective and support.

Obtain and use correct knowledge about the workings of the psyche. Tap into the mind's potential to uncover what is false and its potential to turn attention to What is True. For unclear knowledge, excessive theory or excessive belief keeps the mind spinning in circles with no resolution to the deepest questions.

Observe it all without judgment or expectation, and do not demand perfection, for demanding perfection is a misuse of the intellect. If there is judgment or expectation, observe the judgment and the expectation.

At the times when suffering lifts, give freely to yourself and others, for that is the natural and rightful work of the mind, heart, and body, but primarily the heart. Again, without expectation. And if there is expectation, observe it.

The rest will take care of itself, and one may find that there is
Nothing Wrong and that the Freedom one seeks is pervading
one's daily life.

– DO WE PREPARE THE HOUSE
FOR THE ARRIVAL OF THE MASTER?

Yes, that is a good analogy with a caveat, as must be the case with all analogies.

The house is the personality and the body. The arrival of the Master is the event of the Realization of our True Nature. If the house is in good shape, the Master can stay and live there. Otherwise, the Master cannot.

First, the basic physical needs and stability must be addressed. Then, there must be sufficient psychological maturity and strength, that is, sufficiently free from false beliefs, false ideas (imagination), and negative emotions, and a degree of detachment must be present.

Then, if Awakening occurs and the house is clean, it can "stick." If the personality is "dirty," the Truth of Awakening will not stick. The Master will buzz off. Like surfaces do not stick together if there is dust or dirt between them.

It is common for an Awakening to occur before Spiritual Realization settles. It is a glimpse for the seeker.

The Awakening reveals what the seeker is seeking. Until then, the work was all done in the dark based either on idealized spiritual goals for a "me" that never existed in the first place.

If the personality is still unbalanced, the Glimpse remains a memory, and then more work is required until the personality is clean enough. Then, Spiritual Realization can occur.

After the Glimpse, the process of elimination and cleanup becomes a priority, fueled by the seeker's desire to see the process through.

The caveat of the analogy is that the "arrival of the Master" is not something in the future. No Master arrives. No real "I" arrives. The Real never went anywhere, and you were never separate from It. That is the limitation of the analogy.

Due to the very nature of the mind and identification, the seeker will inevitably project liberation into the future. After all, suffering is present and does not go away, so we must hope and project that, at some point, it will not be there. But that perspective can change.

What Is Being Sought is here and now. Always and everywhere. That is the crux of the whole drama.

– WHAT DO YOU MEAN BY "LOVE, TRUTH, AND BEAUTY?"

When the mind is stable and free from time-induced restlessness, there is no rejection of what is in the moment; there is a profound acceptance or welcoming of What Is, thus, love.

Upon the realization of Who We Are, the True Nature of the universe is also known – known to be no different or separate from What I Am: Consciousness, thus truth.

When the mind is not resisting what is in the moment, it spontaneously creates joy and shares joy, thus beauty.

Such trinity corresponds to the natural operation of the three centers of sentient beings: emotional, intellectual, and physical.

A normal person lives in love, truth, and beauty. In Tarot, that is represented by the card "The World".

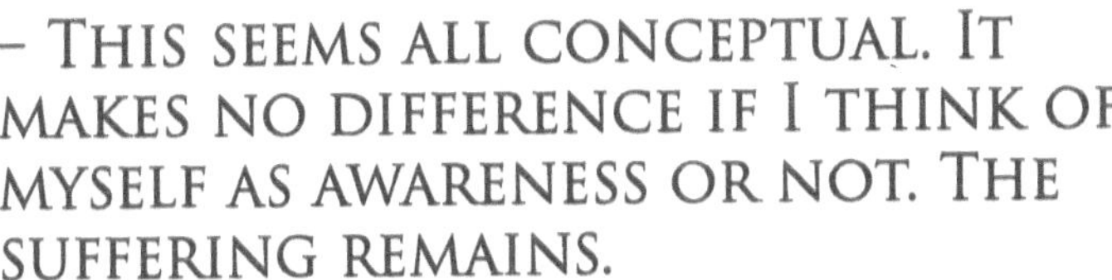

– THIS SEEMS ALL CONCEPTUAL. IT MAKES NO DIFFERENCE IF I THINK OF MYSELF AS AWARENESS OR NOT. THE SUFFERING REMAINS.

It certainly is all conceptual. However, the concepts point beyond the conceptual in a gamble that our sight may turn that way.

Thinking is not all equal. Some thinking supports the ego's sense of separation. Some thinking invites Truth and is a reflection of Truth.

The ego was conditioned to think we are the body and the personality. That is a deeply built-in assumption that most people never question. And along with a heavy emotional charge, it supports the ego's sense of separation.

What I am doing here is offering concepts that spur questioning of the deep untruths we carry in our psyches.

As for whether thinking makes a difference or not, that is totally out of my and your hands. In fact, understanding that it is out of our hands can already significantly impact the degree of suffering experienced. It may, in fact, eliminate the suffering because individual powerlessness is in itself a facet of Truth. And Truth sets us free.

John Wheeler told me that I am the Sky and that the ego and the body are clouds. Hearing that had a crucial role to play in the Awakening that took place shortly after. And the Truth pointed at then remains the source of peace in my daily life.

– It seems that Enlightenment produces clarity about life...

Clarity is one of the manifested dimensions of the Natural State. Clarity is Truth. Enlightenment probably would not be called Enlightenment if it weren't.

But once Awakening or Enlightenment occurs, a new process usually begins in the personality. Enlightenment rarely happens, and we are free from suffering out of the bat. A process of elimination, healing, and re-education is necessary.

Although mental clarity and eloquence are not synonymous with Enlightenment, clarity of thought is an asset in the processes before and after Enlightenment.

– Until final realization happens..."

The concept of final realization keeps the seeker seeking and tied to time instead of looking into the present for what matters. It is a mental cul-de-sac. It does not promote clarity at all.

You cannot think of a final realization, think you are a seeker and perform Inquiry simultaneously. You either feed the seeking by thinking, "You are not there," and "Will realize one day," or you turn your attention to Our Real Nature right now.

If that becomes impossible, we must backtrack and look at false personality more closely because certain things are still unconscious. There is no mystery. These are all known patterns.

False personality has ideas about what Awakening and Spiritual Realization are, and those ideas are built on false personality's fears. So, it projects those fears into the event or state of Enlightenment or Realization. We have to see and understand our imaginary fears so that they may be discarded. There is no shortcut.

— Or we simply let go of the whole thing..."

Well, that would be a shortcut! The question remains: can you do that by choice and will?

If letting go happens, great! Let's go and have a party instead of talking about this stuff... If that does not occur, looking and scrutinizing the mind can be very effective. The mind is equipped to undo its self-undoing.

Some thoughts feed false personality; others are neutral, and others assist the Inquiry and investigation. Some degree of discrimination must be present to discern. That is when mental clarity is helpful and needed.

– CAN'T THE EGO LEARN TO BEHAVE IN A HEALTHY WAY?

It learned to behave badly in the past. If the desire and the conditions are present it can certainly get a new and wiser education. Thankfully.

When we see clearly that we are not the image we have been programmed to believe we are and see the body for what it really is—a present perception or experience—the ego naturally and spontaneously begins to operate more healthily, to the degree that false beliefs are eliminated and no longer followed. Certain stimuli are removed, so specific responses are also removed.

Focus on recognizing what is false and eliminating what is useless, and everything else will fall into place gracefully.

However, don't expect perfection. The notion that we will become as sweet as honey, masters of our thoughts and emotions, or become like Buddha or whoever we have elevated to a spiritual pedestal may be inspiring, but ultimately, it is spiritually misguided. A certain number of people may actually behave like Mother Teresa because that is what their souls and personalities are attuned to. For others, this is not the case.

Each personality is uniquely programmed in terms of traits and depth. Moreover, each soul is unique and has its focus, traits, history, and age, shaped through many physical lives. Even though what unites us all is One, each individual manifests Spiritual Realization differently.

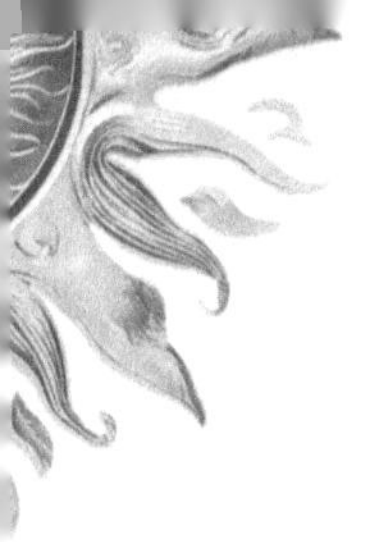

Buddha was the incarnation of a soul so ancient that its manifestation is unfathomable to us. His conscious manifestation goes far beyond the physical realm. If we met him, we would perceive a mere fraction of his being.

For some people, certain unpleasant traits are eradicated. For others, they are perceived as passing clouds. The Peace of Total Acceptance arising from the Natural State means total acceptance of the experience at this moment. No projection and no perfection are required.

– Is Prayer Useful?

If you do not tie your camel and it runs away, and then you pray for its recovery, you may well get your camel back. But if you ignore your negligence, you will not gain anything substantial. Chances are you will lose your camel again.

Suppose you pray for deliverance from suffering but remain unconscious of your self-undoing and justify all kinds of false ideas, theories and beliefs, and self-centered negative emotions. In that case, prayer is useless and can even backfire. No god will give you peace if the devil runs free in your unattended garden.

Prayer can be used as a type of meditation. You focus your attention on an idea and attempt to draw the Wisdom behind it. Self-remembering or self-inquiry is one such practice.

Take the first line of St. Francis' prayer, for example: "Lord, make me an instrument of Thy peace."

Focus on the peace, and if it is revealed, the prayer will have worked on its deepest level. If the Lord's Peace is Known, the Self is Known. It all points to the same Thing. It invites Awakening.

— But in the language of these prayers, there is a separation between God and me!

These prayers can be helpful before Awakening. Afterward, they make no sense because direct experience confirms that there is no separation.

It is the same with mystic poets. They say, "Don't go back to sleep," and "the Friend." Well, You were never awake and never asleep, and there is no separate "Friend."

With Awakening, it is known in direct experience that there is no me here and a "Friend" there. So prayers and exaltations to God become meaningless and are naturally discarded. That process gives room to a deeper relationship with Divinity, which culminates at any moment with the Dissolution of such a relationship.

– And it is in dying that we are born to eternal life." I suppose that refers to the death of the ego.

That refers to the dissolution of the sense of separation. That manifestation of the ego ceases, and thus, Eternal Being becomes evident.

The notion of dying into eternal life after physical death, which is prevalent in certain religions, is a fantastic misinterpretation and distortion of once genuine spiritual teachings.

Spiritual Realization has no relation to the death of the physical body. It relates to, or is equal to, the death of the sense of separation. Nothing more.

– IS MEDITATION USEFUL?

What is meditation? It is to spend time paying attention to something or some process.

Meditation to inquire into who experiences states, that is, the Subject of experience, may lead to Awakening, which means the revelation of uninterrupted peace beyond the pendulum, with no compulsion for experiencing or searching for this or that state.

Meditation, or "paying attention," is vital in observing and analyzing the psyche and eliminating what is useless and harmful.

There is evidence that meditation can be helpful for other purposes, too. It depends on what one wants and on one's degree of understanding.

– SCIENCE WILL UNDERSTAND CONSCIOUSNESS ONE DAY…

Science will understand the dimensions of manifested consciousness, explore and expand it, and create incredible things and experiences. That includes creating fixes for the body and mind to promote well-being.

Science will not understand Pure Consciousness or the Source of Manifestation. This is not because science is somehow faulty or because science-inclined individuals lack intention or ability, but because it simply does not apply; it is apples and oranges.

Having said that, the word "consciousness" has different meanings depending on the context in which it is used.

As for the meaning of Consciousness as a spiritual pursuit, the only thing that matters is the cessation of unnecessary suffering, as far as I am concerned.

The science of psychology can help with that. The different processes addressed by psychology and their relation to spirituality are eloquently described in the Marseilles Tarot, and the patterns of unnecessary suffering are sharply outlined in the Michael Teachings' Overleaves System.

– Is a teacher necessary for Spiritual Realization?

There are no rules. The teacher in the form of a person is only one of many possible.

A person who is a teacher, can provide consistent intellectual articulation and emotional resonance. Human interaction is special because of empathy. The teacher has lived the suffering the seeker is living through. In the case of Spiritual Realization, the teacher understands in direct experience how the end of suffering comes about.

– What other forms are possible?

It depends on the focus, depth and breath of awareness we are endowed with, and our ability to read the messages. Tarot, telepathic connection with guides, channeling, books, videos, and audio are all possible teachers.

If Awakening has already happened, one knows "where one is going," so help will come to lead one in the direction of finalizing the process of dissolution of falseness.

If it has not happened, the pointers will show us what we must see to strengthen our true personality and prepare for Awakening.

Our husband or wife can be a teacher. A friend, the beggar in the street, the cashier at the supermarket, our pet, the sky, a flower, the oil spill on the pavement, anything teaches.

The less self-centered fear there is, the more powerful teachers become available.

Being conscious itself is a teacher. In a state of enough sensitivity, everything is teaching us something at all times.

I read somewhere that the sage Milarepa gave an interesting answer to that question. He said, "I have twenty-eight teachers, including the four elements."

That means he was in a state of un-involvement with the ego such that anything in his life was pointing the way, and he could hear it.

In the last stages of the spiritual path, there is no hierarchy. Teacher and student are equals. Their difference lies only in the fact that one suffers unnecessarily, and the other doesn't. So, the one who isn't suffering does what they can to assist the other.

– THERE ARE NO PROOFS OF ANYTHING SPIRITUAL, ONLY BELIEFS.

I agree in part. The essence of Spirit is not any "thing" or experience; thus, it cannot be measured, demonstrated, or proven. When considering Spirit, the only verb that can approach it is the verb to be. This perspective has the potential to bypass the conceptual mind and gives you a chance to "realize" the Spirit's True Nature directly. The idea of Spirit, or the Natural State, is a mere empty concept otherwise.

The moment we objectify Spirit or the Natural State as a concept, we set ourselves separate from it in our minds. That fundamental imagination keeps the seeker seeking and is obliterated when Realization occurs. Spiritual Realization is not a conceptual understanding. The ripe seeker requires a different approach, a specific type of inquiry.

As for beliefs, Spirit is ever available, present, and "realizable." Therefore, for some people, Spirit is not a belief or a mere concept. In Realization, all of our previous beliefs about who we are vanish. We see ourselves for what we are and others for what they are—not merely the personality, not even a soul, but Spirit.

This is not some grandiose state; it is the Natural State of a human being—a three-year-old lives like this. Our minds simply have been filled with wrong ideas and negative emotions in the course of our "education" and conditioning in life so that we have lost sight of what is Natural and thus lost the tranquility that the Natural State implies.

– Tell me why Conscious Unity has any value whatsoever for Earth living!

If by Conscious Unity you mean a mere idea without any reference to an underlying uncontrived and benevolent state of being or some tangible quality that you know to be valuable, then it would be rather useless.

But if we use the term in the way I am using it, then what I am calling "Spirit" or the Natural State is the source of unwavering wisdom, peace, compassion, and beauty for oneself first of all. Then, it quietly radiates those qualities to anyone you come into contact with—your family, friends, and the entire world.

You tell me what value that has on a planet dominated by a suffering, immature, and destructive species like ours.

"The sense of separation is the root of
psychological suffering. The root of
psychological suffering is not lack of
money, time, friends, attention, coffee,
sex, knowledge, experiences of higher
consciousness, eternal life,
or anything else."

- METAPHYSICS -

Distinctions between Spirituality, Metaphysics, and Psychology

My definitions are as follows:

Spirituality is the pursuit of Spirit or the Natural State. Through the realization of Spirit, ignorance and suffering end. The Natural State does not evolve or change but is the source of all change and unchanging inner peace.

Metaphysics is the study and experience of the multiple realities the human mind can experience. There are many levels within metaphysics. The soul is a metaphysical body and the vehicle of experience and expression within the metaphysical manifestation and the physical manifestation when a physical body is created. The soul evolves and changes; thus, it is said that the soul's goal is experiencing, learning, creation, and evolution.

Psychology is the study of the human personality and its components and functions. For the purpose of Spiritual psychological work, the part of the mind that requires special attention is lying, wrong ideas, wrong beliefs, and negative emotions stemming from them—the study of false personality.

While not a strict rule, it is common for spiritual seekers to become interested in and actively involved with metaphysics on their spiritual path.

Once the seeker experiences the pleasures and power of metaphysical realities while on the physical plane, they often desire to go back "there" after they come down from the high.

Around that experience, the belief often arises and is frequently preached that Spiritual Realization is equal to a metaphysical experience that is to be found in a higher state of consciousness.

This can become a significant false belief a seeker experiences on the path and become a detour or cul-de-sac.

It may also happen that a genuine insight into the Natural State is misinterpreted, giving rise to the false belief that it is something that "I" can achieve.

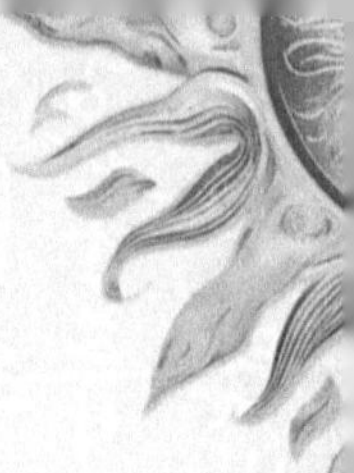

– WHAT DO YOU MEAN BY HEAVEN, HELL AND PURGATORY?

Those are esoteric symbols. Hell is the state where the false personality is active and runs our lives. It is a state full of psychological suffering, fear, uneasiness, and restlessness.

Heaven is our natural state of peace and absolute acceptance.

Purgatory is the mental-emotional process we go through on the path from hell to heaven; it may take the form of "spiritual/psychological work."

The Tarot of Marseilles describes that process and provides insight as to what to pay attention to at each step along the way.

Some psychological teachings mention heaven or paradise and state that you will get there one day. That may be encouraging earlier on the path to gather strength.

However, you will not get there. There is no "you" who gets anywhere. And heaven is not "there"; it is not "here" either. It is Omnipresence, just like Jesus's original teaching states.

Heaven is not the state when "we" are present. Such an idea perpetuates the notion of a self that is unenlightened or asleep and can awaken or become enlightened. It is all notional.

Heaven is not fireworks, excitement, metaphysical powers, visions, or encounters with angels; it is not higher centers.

Heaven is the calm of Being. It is a state of being where involvement with an image of self and its fears is absent. Heaven is Consciousness without any qualifications. And no one and nothing exists apart from it. It is not a special state. It is utter Simplicity; thus, it is also called the Natural State.

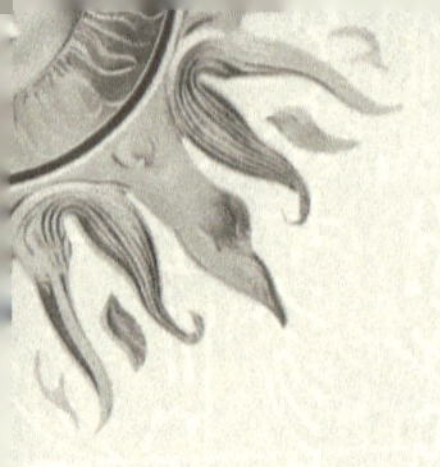

HIGHER CENTERS

— "Lower functions have a dual aspect of positive and negative. The higher emotional and higher intellectual centers do not have that duality."

The "non-duality" of higher centers is a "relative non-duality" and is still part of Duality. Duality is the "ten thousand things". The manifestation. The universe. Subject-object. Perceiver-perceived. Experience.

We are mixing different concepts from different traditions while using the same term. These traditions describe different models, and they are not interchangeable.

The term "Non-duality" means something different in Non-Duality teachings compared to metaphysically oriented teachings.

Duality exists in all planes and all centers. "Non-Dual Truth," as expounded by Buddha, Lao Tzu, Jesus, Nisargadatta, Ramana, and many others, has no relation to planes of existence or with centers higher or lower. The realization of what is transcendent of those "centers" and the multitude of experiences they provide is equal to Non-Dual Truth.

The planes of existence are Duality. The evolution and ascension of the soul are Duality. Any experience or perception, higher or lower, is Duality.

The Realization of Non-Duality is not dependent on higher centers and is always available and present.

– WHEN YOU REFER TO SPIRIT, ARE YOU TALKING ABOUT THE SOUL?

No. The soul is something associated with "me." Spirit is beyond "me" of any kind, physical or metaphysical.

In my definition, Spiritual Realization is not the creation, salvation, improvement, or evolution of the soul.

Spiritual Realization is the Realization of what we are: Spirit or Pure Consciousness.

Time is needed for the soul to evolve. A soul is an object in duality, just like the physical body.

Spiritual Realization is Timelessness. Spirit is non-dual.

Spiritual Realization is equal to the removal of a false belief. That belief is that we are a body, a personality, or a soul.

We do not become Spirit or return to Spirit. We Are Spirit; we have just been confused until Realization happens.

– IS NOT THE SOUL ON A PATH THROUGH MANY LIFETIMES AND IT EVOLVES THAT WAY?

Yes, metaphysical insight or deep intuition reveals that to be the case.

Just like the body and personality change and evolve in their way during this physical lifetime, the soul, or a metaphysical body, evolves through multiple lifetimes.

However, Spiritual Realization does not concern itself with the evolution of the soul. In fact, such concern can become an obstacle.

A concern with the salvation of "me," whether it is "me" personality, "me" body, or "me" soul, becomes an obstacle for the simple reason that there is no such "me" to be found except as an ephemeral experience of individuality.

Thus, concern for the soul's future strengthens the ego's sense of separation. It does nothing to put an end to psychological suffering—quite the contrary.

– DO WE CREATE A SOUL AND ACHIEVE ETERNAL LIFE?

The body enables the experience of life day by day in the physical realm. The soul allows for the same, lifetime by lifetime, alternating between the physical and the astral, a metaphysical realm.

Spiritual Realization, or the Realization of and living as Who We Are, has nothing to do with the body, the soul, or "you" of any kind. It has nothing to do with either physics or metaphysics. And it is not meant to be achieved after traversing metaphysical realms; it is available now.

To Spirit, the notions of birth or death are of no consequence. There have been many, and there may be a few more. There is no one to care.

The notion of immortality can only appeal while the sense of separation is in full force.

Wouldn't it be wonderful if "I" lived forever? (Preferably without all of my bad habits and illnesses!)

It is an egocentric pursuit. Awakening puts an end to such imaginary spiritual goals.

What is eternal, we already are. We can safely leave the body, the personality, and the soul out of this.

– Nobody can know that reincarnation exists!

You may speak for yourself, but not for everybody.

To say that something does not exist simply because we lack experience or proof is the sin of skeptics. If we do not know, we simply acknowledge we do not know. That keeps the mind open, and then we may learn new things. In this case, we learn that the manifestation is much, much richer than our limited physical reality demonstrates.

Countless people have metaphysical experiences and direct knowledge. This does not contradict the Realization of our True Nature, and while metaphysics can become an obstruction in some instances, in other cases, it can help.

You know how old you are, and you are aware of and knowledgeable about the things you have experienced and the changes your personality, character, and body have undergone in this lifetime.

Likewise, there is a subtler aspect of our manifestation as individuals with a similar perspective of experience through multiple lives. This personality and this name die with this body, but a subtler "person" persists.

The end of the cycle of incarnations has no causal relation to Spiritual Realization or vice versa. The realization of our True Nature is independent and unrelated to those experiences,

although maturity and wisdom gained through time certainly impact whether it happens in this lifetime or not.

When we talk about the "ripeness of the seeker," we are talking about soul maturity. It is the soul that is ripe, not merely this passing personality. It is a much deeper, broader, and substantial part of our being that invites and is "ripe" for Awakening and Realization.

We need to be a little observant to notice that different people have different soul ages. There is no time in one lifetime to grow from the most ignorantly behaving person to the wisest sage. If we can set aside our overly intellectual compass for a moment, we will notice that this can be taken as evidence that our lives are much longer and richer than only this lifetime.

The focus of spiritual work is this lifetime alone, or, to be more specific, this moment alone. How could it be otherwise? This is it. However, the notion that only this one lifetime is available to allow us to go from immaturity to Love, Truth, and Beauty is unrealistic in my view.

Karma is a Name for the Law of "Cause-and-Effect."

If you flick that switch on the wall (cause), the light will go on (effect). That is all Karma means in essence.

However, that law operates on the emotional level, and its implications extend across lifetimes.

Every action elicits a reaction. Most actions and reactions happen quickly, and cause and effect are balanced rapidly.

For example, you steal from someone, and by doing that, you have decreased or destroyed certain possibilities in the victim's life. Later on, you may repent and decide to apologize and pay back. So you can go and return what you stole to the rightful owner. In an ideal scenario, they forgive you, you forgive yourself, and the parties involved live happily thereafter, holding no more accounts with one another.

If you don't pay back, you will feel you owe them, and that feeling will not leave you. Guilt will plague you until the debt is paid. The payment can be made within one lifetime, as in the example I just gave you. If not, it will come up in a future lifetime.

The property you stole (cause) is returned in a future lifetime (effect). The crime (cause) creates guilt (effect). The payment (cause) creates opportunity (effect). Forgiveness (cause) creates peace (effect).

If Karma of a high emotional intensity is not paid, we cannot live in peace. The death of the physical body does not imply a balancing of accounts. So, dying does not bring peace in this case. Writing R.I.P. on a tombstone is sweet but futile to those who owe or feel they owe, and for those who feel they are owed.

Karma implies spiritual work, not a spiritual vacation. In the presence of unpaid Karma and the absence of spiritual work, we live in hell, and there is little or no progress.

Forgiving oneself for our transgressions is also needed, as it is possible to accrue Karma with oneself through extreme guilt.

Extreme manifestations of false personality destroy opportunities for ourselves because extreme fear limits our actions and expressions in life. So, self-karma is created—or paid—when false personality is neutralized, we live in fearlessness and express our natural talents.

PATTERNS IN THE SPIRITUAL PATH THROUGH THE LENS OF MARSEILLES TAROT

Besides being a method of communication with metaphysical realms of the manifestation to obtain information, the Marseilles Tarot is a system of psychological delineation capable of describing the patterns of experience humans encounter on the physical plane, including the spiritual path.

This abbreviated sequence of images from the Marseilles Tarot Major Arcana corresponds to the key milestones in the conscious spiritual path.

PREPARATORY WORK

Observation and assessment of our past and present decisions and experiences. Shaping and control of the detrimental or unruly parts of our personalities. Efforts. The early stages of psychological or spiritual work.

AWAKENING

The True Self Revealed. 1 am not what 1 thought 1 was. 1 am Consciousness. We are powerless as individuals, yet profound Acceptance and freedom exist in that powerlessness. Our view of self and the world are turned upside-down. Mountains are not mountains, rivers are not rivers...

ELIMINATION

This card does not have a name—it indicates that attachment to all symbols of self-identity must go. We are now transitioning out from being oppressed by a false personality. Something in our ego is dying; by the end of this process, that something will be dead.

SELF-INQUIRY

The act of questioning and investigating the origin of thoughts, sensations, and emotions. Questioning or paying attention to "who I am." Self-inquiry. We are stripped of all intention for Enlightenment and knowledge. Consciousness is calling itself and hearing itself. Self-remembering.

SPIRITUAL REALIZATION

Nothing is wrong anymore. Total Acceptance and peace with whatever is present at this moment. We have the resources needed to meet the requirements of life. There is nothing to hide, be fearful of, or fearful for. Mountains are again seen as mountains, and rivers as rivers.

For a complete analysis of the spiritual path through the lens of the Marseilles Tarot Major Arcana visit hangedmanspath.com.

– ASTROLOGY JUST TELLS
A STORY ABOUT THE PERSON...

It depends on what kind of astrology. To begin with, the sun-sign astrology that most people know nowadays is a limited, distorted, and often banalized version of the traditional astrology that has been practiced for millennia. So, most people do not know the various branches of astrology and what real astrology is or can do.

As for it "just" telling a story, it depends on who uses it.

Real astrology offers a model that is a diagram of the human personality and its relation to what is beyond the personality.

If we want to heal the psyche, real astrology can be very helpful. It can give us a practical description of what the personality is made of and what is going on with it. It helps us see things as they are. Thus, is can help us understand and deal with challenges in any area of our lives, including spirituality

Some seekers seem to think that healing is not necessary. Well, if trauma remains unseen and certain karma unpaid, the peace of Realization does not stick. There is no way around that.

Awakening is not the end for most. It is the beginning of the end. The psyche needs to be healthy for that which was "discovered" in Awakening to shine through. For the Moon (personality) to reflect the light from the Sun (Spirit).

So, if we want to tell entertaining stories or know astrologers who like to spin stories, we can use astrology to do that.

If we want to understand the human psyche and its proclivities —both those that support and those that obstruct Awakening and Spiritual Realization, we can do that too by using a tool like Traditional Astrology.

– GLOSSARY –

EGO
The sense of self that allows us to function in the physical world. An uneducated or imbalanced ego can lead to the formation of a false personality where psychological suffering is created.

PERSONALITY
The broader set of psychological traits that form a person, and through which the sense of self, or ego, manifests.

SENSE OF SEPARATION
Attachment to, or involvement with, the entity that goes by our name, and the personal feeling of being separate from the rest of the universe, and the feeling of vulnerability that it generates. The sense of separation is the root of psychological suffering.

PSYCHOLOGICAL / UNNECESSARY SUFFERING
Suffering that is created based on wrong identification. Suffering created through false personality. If the wrong ideas are recognized and neutralized, and the identification is corrected, psychological suffering becomes absent.

FALSE PERSONALITY
That part of our personalities that, when active, produces psychological suffering. Usually, the ego does not receive proper education early in life, and thus, fear becomes overblown, and psychological suffering becomes habitual.

ACCUMULATION
The process a seeker goes through in the early phase of spiritual work whereby the ego is re-educated, observed, and controlled. During this period, the seeker does not know what they are seeking or has a vague intuition about it.

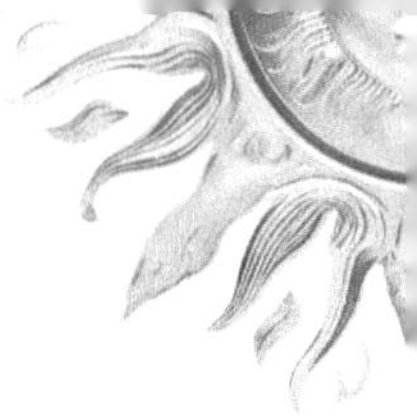

AWAKENING / REVELATION / ENLIGHTENMENT

A recognition of our True Nature and the world's True Nature
as One. That is, All is Consciousness.

ELIMINATION

The process a seeker goes through in the final period of spiritual
work, whereby the personality is stripped of unnecessary
concepts, beliefs, and functions. This period begins with
Awakening. In this period, the seeker has a clear, intuitive
knowledge, based on direct experience, of what they are seeking.

SELF-INQUIRY / SELF-REMEMBERING

The act of investigating the True Nature of "I," or questioning
the veracity of "I." Before Awakening, this action may lead to
Awakening. After Awakening, this action has the function of
re-establishing the Truth glimpsed and contributing to further
eliminating the unnecessary from the seeker's personality.

SPIRITUAL REALIZATION

Total Acceptance and peace with whatever is present at this
moment. Absence of sense of separation. Absence of psychological
suffering and seeking. Nothing is wrong anymore.

I AM

Space and the sense of existing prior to having a name, a
personality, or a body. It is the seed of the manifestation or
experience. It is the Natural State manifested in sentient form.

SPIRIT / NATURAL STATE / PURE CONSCIOUSNESS

Our Natural State is realized when the sense of separation is
removed. Our True Nature is not something special that is
reached or achieved, it is natural and normal. Now.

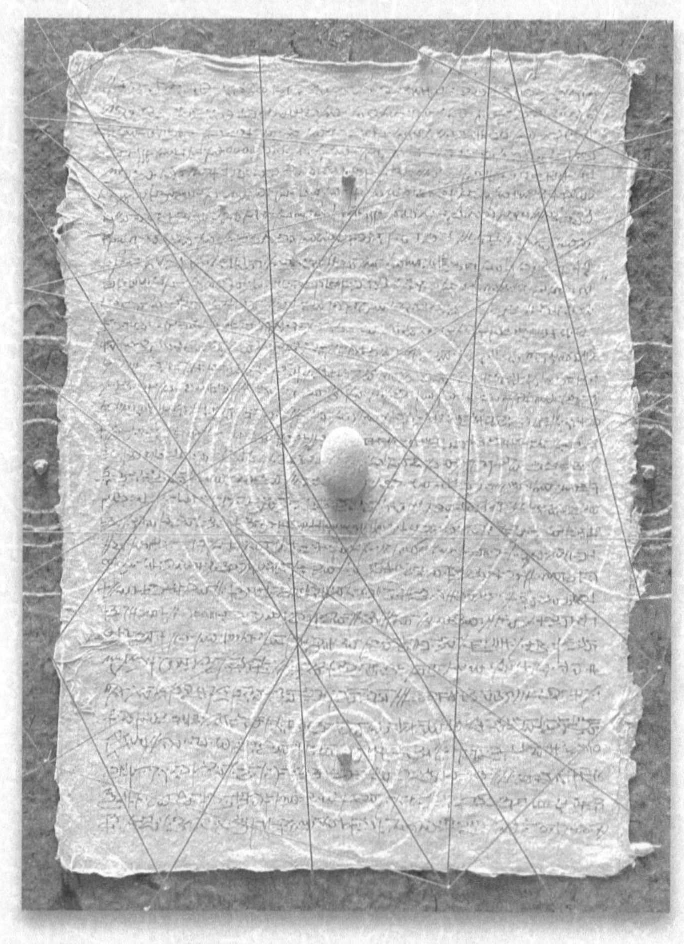

Detail of "Inner Geometry"

MIXED MEDIA BY CARLOS GRASSO
carlosgrasso.com